For the people of the clay country, whose generosity, spirit and commitment to their community are an inspiration to us all and without whom, this book would not have been possible.

And to Bernhard Ray, the man who made the clay trails happen. Thanks for singing with us in the Eden Choir and for making this very special, secret part of Cornwall so accessible.

You never saw
The clay as I have seen it, high
On the bare hills, the little breasts
So white in the sun, all the veins running white
Down to the board womb with its scars

by Jack Clemo

2

"We call the tips burras - we live at Caudledown Lane, it was so beautiful up there until they pulled down all the burras." Jenny Carter, Treverbyn.

"I used to drive for heavy transport. When I'd come back home over Bodmin Moor, all I remember seeing was all those tips with the sun in the background. Bowaters was the first one you'd come to, drive a little further and they'd cover the horizon." Des Carter, Treverbyn.

3

"...It was on this high plateau, encompassing White Moor and Hensbarrow Downs, eastward to Luxulyan and St Austell, west to Goss Moor and Indian Queens, that one William Cookworthy, a Plymouth Quaker, founded the china clay industry, absorbing into it many tin-workers in the district who through lack of work found themselves in distress.

Today the industry is the greatest in all Cornwall...

... the industrial area, roughly some twenty-five miles in circumference, is a world of its own...

Bugle, Stenalees, Foxhole, Nanpean, Treviscoe, St Stephen-in-Brannel, St Dennis, these were villages or scattered hamlets once, and have developed solely on account of china clay, housing the majority of its workers...

...The men are specialists, brought up to clay from birth, second and third generation, and, like the tinners before them, have the same sense of solidarity..."

Daphne du Maurier, *Vanishing Cornwall.*

This book could not have been written were it not for the strong sense of solidarity Daphne du Maurier notes in her 1967 publication, *Vanishing Cornwall*. The great thing is that there's nothing vanishing about the sense of solidarity in Cornwall's clay.

Pit-worker's jobs may have disappeared and entire villages have been buried under the area's mountainous waste tips, but the sense of community, togetherness and solidarity that exists within the clay villages, I'm not so sure that's going to vanish anywhere!

Solidarity is something that's been dug very deeply into the people of the St Austell uplands - it's a quality that's helped clay workers pull together and dig the deepest of pits with their bare hands and then play out their hearts at the local band club. It's given clay working families the strength of each other in times of extreme hardship and galvanised villages in the face of uncertainty and change.

We've been fortunate to experience the solidarity and generous hearts of many individuals and groups in the clay.

We're incredibly grateful for the support, funding and sponsorship we have received from Feast, the China Clay Local Action Group, the Eden Project, St Austell Brewery, Imerys, the China Clay History Society and Wheal Martyn.

Furthermore, an enormous thank you to the many individuals and schoolchildren, too numerous to mention, who have made a clay figure, shared a memory or two, offered up their photo collection and taken time to talk to us or participate in the community activities we've run.

And, in the spirit of any clay country event, many of our friends and family have gone over and above the call of duty to help and support us as we've attempted to create a colourful little book and touring exhibition The Fifty Shades of Clay. You all know who you are and we'd like to thank you too.

Cornwall's clay country is a world of its own and we feel incredibly privileged to have spent time in that world; in the various village halls, Sunday schools, working men's clubs, churches, front rooms, classrooms, kitchens, gardens, even greenhouses. Thank you for having us.
Emma and Tom

"This part of Cornwall might well be called a 'white country'. For everything here *is* white. The dumps are white, the streams look like milk, there are pools and tanks of white water, and great stacks of white clay.

The men themselves, as you see them coming home from their work, look as if they had been rubbing powdered chalk over their faces and hands."
The Story of Cornwall, **A. K. Hamilton Jenkin, 1934.**

Did you know?

China clay is a fine white powder used in the paper, ceramics, coatings and pharmaceuticals industries.

China clay was originally discovered in China (funny that!).

Its technical name kaolin comes from the Chinese word *Kauling*, meaning 'high ridge'. Kauling is also the name of the village near Jingdezhen, Jiangxi province, China, where white clay was first extracted for use in Chinese porcelain.

China clay was first discovered in Cornwall in 1746 at Tregonning Hill, near Helston by William Cookworthy, a chemist from Devon.

Cornwall's china clay has been quarried from opencast mines for over 260 years.

Cornwall's clay has been nicknamed 'white gold' (with an annual turnover of over £100 million a year it's no wonder).

China clay is such a versatile and useful substance that almost every household in the western world is home to a product containing china clay (even if it's just toothpaste).

Created by the Royal Crown Derby just over a century ago, the porcelain tableware made for the *Titanic* was fired using Cornwall's very own porcelain-grade white clay. It was quarried by the Martin Brothers from the pit at Treviscoe.

The Wheal Martyn China Clay Museum and Country Park, which opened in 1975, is dedicated to telling the story of china clay production in Cornwall and its amazing history.

Wheal Martyn is the only museum in the world where you get to view a working china clay pit and can see the largest working water wheel in Cornwall!

The old clay works, which form part of the museum, began extracting clay during the 1820s – today the buildings are a scheduled monument.

The museum's 'Pit to Port' tour takes you right down into the heart of a working clay pit so you can experience at first hand the clay extraction process as it gets washed from the pits above St Austell to being shipped from the port at Fowey.

After oil, china clay is the United Kingdom's (UK) second largest mineral export. In Cornwall it's the largest (apart from the pasty that is).

China clay is one of the purest forms of clay on the planet and comes from the decomposition of moorland granite. Before its commercial extraction, china clay was known as Moorstone, Growan or Growan clay and used as a local building material.

The clay-bearing ground in mid-Cornwall covers a total area of 25 square miles. It's estimated there are enough reserves of kaolin here for at least another century (and at least a few more generations).

A little less than a century ago, the St Austell uplands witnessed the largest clay strike Cornwall has ever seen.

July 2013 marks the centenary of the Cornish clay strike, an event in which over 5,000 clay workers went on strike for higher rates of pay and better terms and conditions.

The strike action, which started at Carne Stents, Trewoon, began when the clay firm went back on its word to pay workers every fortnight rather than monthly. As the men downed tools, they marched from pit to pit gathering more and more clay workers and production ground to a halt.

The uprising was so strong that the local police force had to draft in especially trained officers from Glamorgan in Wales. The Welsh recruits were selected for being larger in size and had experience working on picket lines.

The strike, as featured in the 1972 television play Stocker's Copper, lasted for 3 months. During a tense and violent time, workers were forced back to the pits as they ran out of money.

"It was an event that rocked the whole community and had profound effects in Cornwall... and the strike helped bolster trade unionism in Cornwall. With nowhere big enough to meet, the union built a number of halls and one of the strike leaders, Joe Harris, became a popular Labour leader." Nigel Costley South West Trade Union Congress.

Even though they were eventually defeated, their protest was not entirely fruitless. A few months later a deal was negotiated offering workers a new three-year pay offer with 25 shillings more than the terms demanded as part of the original strike.

The Hensbarrow uplands are famous for being home to some of the richest kaolin deposits in the world.

After Brown Willy and Roughtor on Bodmin Moor, Hensbarrow Beacon, a mile northwest of Stenalees, is the 3rd highest point in Cornwall.

The natural summit of Hensbarrow is 312m high. However, if you wander up there (and it's well worth it)**, you'll notice that there's an enormous grassy bank towering 42 metres above the trig point. This is of course a giant waste tip – testimony to the epic nature of this industry.**

Hensbarrow Beacon is probably the only place on the planet where you'll find a mountain, made from the by-product of china clay, which knocks the third highest point in the area into fourth position! (perhaps they should call it White Willy)

The granite uplands of mid-Cornwall, whose rock beds gave birth to the British china clay industry, are over 300 million years old. They date back to a time when Cornwall lay somewhere on the equator!

The moorland above St Austell, which has been swallowed entirely by centuries of china clay extraction, would have looked much like Goss and Tregoss Moor, now the largest surviving sections of the mid-Cornwall moors left in the area.

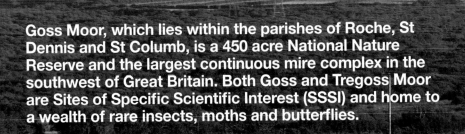

Goss Moor, which lies within the parishes of Roche, St Dennis and St Columb, is a 450 acre National Nature Reserve and the largest continuous mire complex in the southwest of Great Britain. Both Goss and Tregoss Moor are Sites of Specific Scientific Interest (SSSI) and home to a wealth of rare insects, moths and butterflies.

Goss Moor was as a great place to go 'picking smutties' too.

In the days of the steam train, the gorse and dried grass on the moor were often set alight by the sparks from the locomotive's smoke stacks. The gorse never completely burned, it charred and was known locally as 'smutties'. Local people would go out collecting smutties, which made great fuel to heat their water boilers.

Having been a popular gypsy camp and dump for the rubble ruins of Plymouth after the Second World War, Goss Moor is home to the springs, which give rise to the tributaries of the River Fal. The headwaters of the Fal rise in the Coldreath area.

An important supply of water to homes and farmers (and a top spot in times gone by for a quick summer dip) the cleanliness of the River Fal was and still is extremely important. Whilst modern-day clay producers take care not to contaminate the river, in centuries gone by their carelessness contributed to a significant decline in local flora and fauna.

Today, the work of English Nature has helped to restore species populations in the area, making the moors an interesting and very peaceful place to explore (especially without the roar of what was once the A30).

The river running between Hensbarrow and Pentewan, the Winnick, is known in the clay as the White River. Most of the rivers in the area ran white as excess clay from the pits and refineries was released, or trickled its way into local waterways.

In 1962, when the demand for clay was extremely high, the clay companies estimated that over 200,000 tons of saleable clay was being washed into the rivers every year.

"It made paddling at Pentewan and Par a really squishy experience, what with all the mica and clay under your feet." Ivor Bowditch

Holidaymakers enjoying the local coastline would have bathed in the stuff and if you looked out over St Austell Bay, not only were there more ships, but the shallow waters of the shore were white with clay.

"The local catch was whitebait, there were loads of whitebait. We think they thrived because their big fish predators couldn't see them and then eat them, because of all the clay in the water." Dr Colin Bristow

Despite this apparent pollutant, another environmental cost of clay, the memory of St Austell's white water is held very dear in the hearts of clay-working families. The rivers ran white during a time of employment and security. It would never happen now, today the streams run clean.

Nevertheless, if you look carefully after heavy rain, the rivers are sometimes a little creamy and if you take a left and drive down towards Brake Manor, on the road from St Austell to Ruddlemoor, you can still see a faint trace of white clay in the water (powerful stuff).

The stepped hillsides and tips that mark the horizon of mid-Cornwall are entirely man-made. The once white pyramids are mountainous piles of waste rock and earth.

The landscape above St Austell consists of over 450 million tons of waste soil, rock and sand removed over centuries to expose the china clay.

The white pyramids write an interesting signature on the local skyline, provoking mixed feelings amongst locals and visitors.

Some see them as a meaningful mark of a working landscape and its industrial heritage, some see them as offensive and ugly waste tips scarring the area's skyline and others see them as curious, abstract and **exotic** (we love 'em).

Until the 1960s Cornwall's clay country peaks were pyramid shaped. After changes in technology and the Aberfan disaster in Wales, where a tip collapsed killing 116 school children and 28 adults, most of the tips in Cornwall were flattened into the stepped hillsides visible today.

The pyramid-shaped peaks just above the village of St Dennis are affectionately known as flatty and pointy (I wonder why!).

Since its discovery, over 160 million tons of china clay have been extracted from Cornwall.

That's about £16,000,000,000 (yes, that's 16 billion pounds worth).

In comparison, Cornwall's tin and copper industry has grossed about £9 billion in its lifetime.

So, the value of Cornwall's clay is nearly twice that of the sum of its tin and copper counterparts (incredible really).

The world demand for china clay is somewhere in the region of 25 million tons per year. 5% of the world's supply comes from Cornwall and all of that comes from the St Austell area.

This book, just like best-selling *Little Book of Cornwall,* tells the story of Cornwall's clay country through a rich, eclectic and diverse collection of facts, anecdotes and stories.

In comparison to other parts of Cornwall, to me the clay district is the unsung, often uncelebrated hero of the story of Cornwall. The social and economic impact and legacy of mid-Cornwall's china clay industry is epic, truly epic, and equally as significant as that of tin and copper mining – yet the clay area is rarely visited.

Just like the many important minerals discovered in and around the St Austell area, the rural pathways, solid granite villages, isolated hamlets and numerous Methodist chapels and farms are each scattered timelessly. They are valuable, hidden gems. In some parts of the clay, time really has stood still. Many villages retain the same character and characters as Cornwall would have seen over 30 years ago.

"Years ago life was at a much steadier pace than it is today... everybody knew everybody else in the village... This is not quite the same today. Married couples and families are coming and going and men are changing jobs and moving to other areas. Even so, the village way of life is still the same in goodwill as in times of stress and necessity, everyone is willing to help and comfort their neighbours."
Mr Poad, *Documentary on Village Life at Nanpean.*

The almost secret tales and treasures that lie within the communities who've dug the pits and carved the tips of Cornwall's white mountains reveal a very different, perhaps more subtle, tougher yet tighter side of life in one of Britain's best-loved holiday spots. A county known for its surf and sandy beaches, its bright blue sea, ice creams and pasties.

Ironically, clay country is not without its own sand-strewn landscape, stunning views and bright blue pools.

Cornwall's clay country even has its own white water and sandcastles but the sandcastles of the clay have been handmade with pickaxes or dumper trucks – not by the colourful buckets and spades that line Cornwall's beaches in summer.

Indeed, white water runs throughout this district but it doesn't form the giant wave faces for those who come in search of the surf.

No – the white water of the clay flows from the rock face as workers wash out the decomposed feldspar held within the granite vertebrae, which form the backbone of Cornwall.

Here in the clay, the bright blue water and turquoise rock pools are found at the bottom of quarries, disused pits and giant settling tanks. You won't find much sea life but their azure glow often beats the Atlantic's.

And that liquid sapphire sheen that illuminates the lakes; it isn't just a reflection of the sky; it's a mark of the clay industry created by the millions of bluey-green mica particles left in the waste water from winning the clay.

Where the Atlantic rollers and English Channel have carved Cornwall's coastline, a 260-year-old industry has shaped our clay country. It's been the hands of men and women that have given the area all of its colour and contours – not those of Mother Nature.

Indeed Cornwall's white gold has come at a price and the natural landscape has changed irrecoverably.

'A stranger set down upon this spot today, or closer still amongst the slag and shale, white hills either side of him, would think himself a thousand miles from Cornwall, in the canyons of Colorado, perhaps, or the craters on the moon.' Daphne du Maurier.

The clay industry has cut giant craters in the centre of Cornwall; deep, opencast scars which, unlike the invisible mines underground, need much more work to heal. But, that healing process is well underway. With the help of clay companies, volunteers and numerous environmental organisations Mother Nature is reclaiming her land.

Through a series of significant re-landscaping and economic regeneration projects including the Eden Project, the clay and Goss Moor trails, and hoped-for developments for St Austell Bay, Cornwall's clay area has become a world-class example of post-mining regeneration.

Nevertheless, to many, visitors and locals alike, the life and landscape, tales and times of the clay communities are still to be discovered. They certainly need to be shared and celebrated and that's what this book is all about.

It has been an honour to have been awarded funding from Feast and to have had sponsorship from The Eden Project and the China Clay Local Action Group to research and collate this book, but it's not been without its challenges.

It would have been all too easy to get caught up in looking back, adopting an overly romantic nostalgia for the past, a narrative not unfamiliar to communities who now experience a climate of uncertainty born from the boom and bust in Britain's mineral industry

Equally, it could have been all too easy to paint an all too pretty picture of a place that's not always easy on the eye and certainly consists of more than 50 shades of grey!

While I've been collating this book, I've had more cups of tea and eaten more cake and homemade pasties than ever before in my time in Cornwall. I hope what's been gathered, photographed and shared here reflects all the colours of the clay, if not get in touch and tell me what I've missed.

Despite the extraordinary heritage and landscape created by the epic process of quarrying for kaolin, the story of clay country, for me, centres on the word 'community'.

Cornwall's clay has quite literally sculpted its communities. Many villages would not exist were it not for kaolin. The industry has moulded and fired people together, shaping their settlements into tight-knit, solid places. Just like a ceramic pot, more important for the space it creates, rather than its actual form, the clay villages have created communities, bound together by their surroundings.

In the words of Rose Barnecut, the families that live in the clay "live deep not broad".

Rose and her family, like many others in Cornwall's clay country, have lived in the area for many generations. They live close to their kin and love their landscape.

For over two centuries it seems, *Clayland*, as poet Alan Kent puts it, has lived an almost secret life. The 25 square miles of clay-bearing ground which yielded much of the world's white clay, has also fired together self-sufficient villages and communities that still retain their truth, 200 years on. I guess the people of these, once car-less, very isolated villages, have only ever really had each other.

Without a vehicle, travel was and still is challenging within the clay, so villages have created their own worlds and not had to look beyond the next village to get what they need. Perhaps that is why they have survived, the clay villagers know what is important to sustain and how to sustain it; and we can all learn a lesson from that.

Within what might appear to be a desolate, almost decimated, yet industrious landscape, peppered with pebble-dashed domesticity, ancient wooded valleys, Domesday-dated farms, isolated terraces and solid stone villages resides a rich (but not necessarily economically), generous and caring community. One that holds dear the many traditions and customs moulded by their clay-bearing forefathers.

Many choruses have been sculpted from the clay. The area is well known for its choirs, bands, carnivals and carnival queens, feasts and festivals.

"We produce silver bands of world renown... the West of England Bandsmen's Festival is awe-inspiring and brings a lump to every throat when Cornish bands march up through the village of Bugle, as dusk falls, holding aloft their trophies and playing their hearts out to the people-lined streets." Councillor Jackie Bull

Just like tin and copper, Cornwall's white gold, kaolin or china clay has given much to Great Britain and other parts of the world and continues to do so.

Even today china clay is a big component in the paper, ceramic and pharmaceutical industries. Local construction and aggregate firms are still underpinned by the many grades of waste product that come from Cornwall's white mountains.

But right now Cornwall's clay country sits, and far from easily, upon a seat that sees a future of ever-changing development, a seat that looks out over a view that could behold the UK's first large-scale incinerator and one of Britain's first government backed Eco Towns.

For many of the choruses who have their home amidst these proposals – it's hard to sing – especially as they stand, bracing themselves against the drone of development and the apparently forward moving motion of the modern world.

As to what happens to the culture and customs of Cornwall's clay over the next decade or so, only time will tell. All we can do and have tried to do here is capture and celebrate community life as it faces and has faced the changes and challenges of reclaiming the land and reinvigorating the social and financial economy of the area.

"As silence falls on dock or moor, They can not break our granite core."

Roger Bryant from the song Cornish Lads

The story of Cornwall's clay country begins over 300 million years ago when the world was ablaze with volcanoes and our planet's processes were firing the earth.

As molten rock forced its way up to the earth's surface it cooled and crystallised to create granite, much of which forms the spectacular tors and uplands that run between Dartmoor and Land's End, the igneous vertebra of the West Country.

Millions of years later, parts of this granite spine would become, and for no less than two and half centuries, the backbone of the world's china clay industry.

gran·ite/_granit/

Noun:

1) A very hard, granular, crystalline, intrusive igneous rock consisting mainly of quartz, mica, and feldspar and often used as a building material.

2) Used in similes and metaphors to refer to something very hard and impenetrable.

The word granite comes from the Latin _granun_ meaning grain, describing the coarse-grained appearance of this crystalline rock.

Granite is an igneous rock, meaning it has been formed from volcanic activity.

In some parts of the world and over millions of years whilst the mica and quartz crystals in the granite rock have remained unchanged, the white feldspar has decomposed, forming a soft white mineral – known as kaolinite – the main component of what we call china clay.

Technically speaking china clay, or kaolin, is a hydrated aluminium crystalline mineral formed by the hydrothermal decomposition of granite rocks (that's a kind of rotting caused by water to you and me).

Kaolin is represented by the chemical formula $Al_2Si_2O_5(OH)_4$.

Geologists believe that the 'kaolinisation' (or the crumbling) of feldspar came about as a result of two of the earth's processes – hydrothermal activity and the weather (and Cornwall certainly gets a lot of that!).

The hydrothermal process explains that hot chemical-laden gases rising up from earth into the granite rocks caused the feldspar to break into a much softer material.

The weathering process, which came millions of years later, puts kaolinisation down to water. Entering the rock through surface cracks, underground water was heated gradually by the radioactive elements in the granite. This warming process slowly decomposed the soft feldspar into white clay leaving the quartz and mica behind.

For centuries, the Chinese used kaolin to make their famous porcelain china but their recipe remained a secret to the Europeans until the 18th century.

In the late 1740s chemist William Cookworthy discovered kaolinised deposits near Helston on the Lizard and later in the St Stephen's area of St Austell. This was the beginning of the British porcelain industry.

Kaolin was first 'discovered' by William Cookworthy at a mine working in Tregonning, near Helston in 1746. It was first found in the St Austell area in 1748 at Carloggas, near St Stephen.

William Cookworthy was born in 1705 into a Quaker family in Kingsbridge, Devon. He made his name in the ceramics industry from his factory at Coxside, Plymouth by being the first to produce a hard-paste from British china clay.

Up until this time, white clay was imported into Britain from Virginia in the United States. It was Cookworthy who believed it was possible to find the same materials in England and he found it first in Cornwall.

Cookworthy patented his hard-paste product, the result of nearly two decades of research, in 1768 and by 1770 porcelain was in high demand – (seems hard to imagine these days).

The first china clay pits in Cornwall were owned by northern ceramic companies. As production became more complicated and demand increased, local adventurers bought back the pits and sold the clay to the porcelain industry through local agents.

By the mid 1800s, there were over 100 clay pits operating in the St Austell area.

The most famous clay pit in the St Austell area is The Eden Project which opened in 2000. It's probably the most famous clay pit in the world. Up until then Eden's home was known as Bodelva, a clay and aggregate quarry covering 0.5 km², which closed in September 1998.

Bodelva Pit produced a pinkish-red clay, which was famous for giving the *Financial Times* its pinky colour.

With a 160-year history as a working pit, Bodelva sits 15m under the water table and covers 15 hectares. At the bottom, where Eden's ice rink resides, it's 60m deep!

At its peak, Bodelva was providing up to 40,000 tons of kaolin each year – today it's home to one of the most popular visitor attractions in the country. (It's amazing what you can do with a massive hole in the ground!)

During the first two months of Eden's construction it rained every single day (and as the 43 million gallons of rainwater drained into the pit, Eden was splashed across the headlines).

Weighing just slightly more than the air they contain, today the Eden Project's famous biomes are the largest geodesic lean-to conservatories in the world, home to the largest rainforest in captivity.

The site has over 135,000 plants from over 4,500 different species each hand-planted in over 83,000 tons of especially made soil (heaven on earth!).

The Eden Project began as a twinkle in Tim Smit's eye in 1995. In 1996 the first images of the now world-famous biomes emerged (even if it was on the back of a napkin!).

The epic construction project was commissioned in 1998 as one of the Land-mark Millennium projects marking the year 2000. (More about the Eden later).

By 1858, a little less than a century after its discovery, there were 42 clay companies in Cornwall employing some six thousand workers producing over 65,000 tons of porcelain-grade clay every year.

By the end of the 18th century business was booming and continued for over 260 years.

By 1891, Cornwall's annual clay production had exceeded 500,000 tons.

By 1955, it had reached 1 million tons.

By 1964, it had reached a 2 million ton milestone with an annual extraction of 2,007,000 tons.

In 1988, the china clay industry celebrated its highest-ever annual tonnage having produced a staggering 3,277,000 tons of china clay that year!

What makes these figures even more astounding is that to extract just one single ton of china clay a further 9 tons of waste rock and debris are produced.

By its very nature, china clay extraction is both intensive and expensive. The process requires a vast amount of water and power.

The washing and refining process uses 30 million gallons of water every single day, 75% of which is recycled and stored in flooded pits and reservoirs.

(Clay pits are very good at storing water. South West Water has bought two of them, Stannon Lake and Park Lake, on Bodmin Moor. It's converted them into reservoirs for our drinking water and are the fourth and fifth largest reservoirs in the region.)

It's no surprise then that the overall water and energy bill for china clay production in Cornwall is somewhere in the region of £23 million a year!

Today, china clay production is Cornwall's largest industry. Up until November 2012, only two companies extracted the 1 million tons of kaolin exported every year.

Goonvean, opened its first clay workings in 1931. The long-established family business owned by the Boscawens operated five pits in the St Austell area; Greensplat, Prosper, Rostrowrack, Goonvean and Trelavours Downs.

Up until its clay workings were purchased by Imerys in 2012, Goonvean was the largest remaining, privately owned, kaolin producer in the EU.

The company extracts around 200,000 tons of kaolin each year, 90% of which is exported to 50 different countries worldwide. The company also supplies 500,000 tons of aggregates every year, which stay within the UK (and will stay within Goonvean Ltd).

Goonvean's grade of clay is particularly special. They are the only producer able to supply clay products that meet the stringent British, European and US pharmacopoeia standards. (In other words their clay good enough to eat and wear - in face packs and face powders that is.)

Imerys is the largest clay producer in Cornwall. It's the largest china clay extractor in the world! The French-owned company took over The English China Clay Company in 1999. Today Imerys operates 7 pits in the area employing approximately 1,000 local people.

The Imerys-owned Karslake Complex is believed to be the biggest china clay pit in the world, deep enough in parts to hide the London Eye (eye wonder how they'd get it down there).

The oldest china clay quarry in Cornwall is Treviscoe Pit, which opened in 1784. The youngest opened in May 2012.

With a footprint the size of 300 football pitches, the largest clay pit in Cornwall ironically includes a pit called Littlejohns! The pit, which opened in 1830 is still in operation today and has been excavated to a depth of 100m.

Higher Moor New Pit, the first clay pit to open in Cornwall since Old Pound in Nanpean in 1984, has the potential to cover 17 hectares – that's about 23 football pitches and will be excavated to a depth of 70m. The kaolin deposits in the new pit are much closer to the surface, so easier to extract.

'The Company' is a phrase you'll often hear in the clay, ex-pit workers will often talk about 'the Company' and how "the Company took care of it".

'The Company' helped to create the communities. "If anyone in the village needed something the first person you'd ring was the local shift captain and he'd make it happen." Ivor Bowditch

When you look at how the 100 or so pits and tips of the clay industry have altered the landscape of mid-Cornwall and united villagers through work, shared memories and a calendar full of events, you have to remark at the power of 'the Company'.

This particular company was English China Clays or ECLP as most people call it (which stood for English Clays, Lovering and Pochin).

At its peak, ECLP were the largest employers in Cornwall. Over 6,000 people were employed by the clay industry. The Company offered huge job security for a time. Even today, Imerys is still one of the longest serving private employers in the region.

'The Company' built houses. 'The Company' put money towards recreational facilities for families and children. 'The Company' held balls and arranged workers' outings. 'The Company' held celebrations and holidays for retired workers (the guest list so big that they had to empty the bagging warehouse at Drinnick to accommodate everyone).

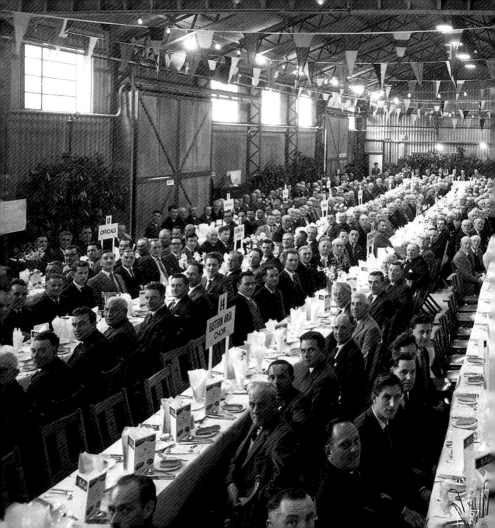

As the ECLP sponsored publications Tales and More Tales from the White Mountains capture, generation after generation worked the pits.

Jobs were passed from grandfather to father and sons would have started as a kettle boy and then worked their way up to shift cap'n, taken a post in the heavy transport division or ended up in other areas of clay production, outside of the pits.

"I was working down Par Moor and every year they would have a new boy come in. What they called a kettle boy. The first day he started he'd come up onto the landing to see if we wanted pasties and that... we used to order pasties from Carne's bakery up St Blazey at that time... Father was the shift captain, he gave me socks for taking the mickey out of the new chap." Hubert Roach

"I was born in 1902, and a job was waiting for me when I left school, and I went to Littlejohns...I was a kettle boy... used to pick up the tea money, y'know thruppence a fortnight...I'd have to carry the tools... dubbers..then I'd have to come back and make tea...

When I got to sixteen I wanted to earn men's pay but the cap'n, he said I'd only get a man's pay when I had done a man's work... Down by Neal's shop, by the big pool, there was a big drag, which collected all the heavy stuff, all the mikee. He said 'you go down there and clean that run of mica... and I'll turn in a man's pay for you, so that's your way to a man's pay." Ray Neal

Just 40 years ago, everyone in the St Austell area would have had a family member employed by ECLP. Even the schoolchildren had a part to play in the clay working day.

"For all those years ago when we was kids Pop worked up Park, mum used to make pasties for us first thing... and we'd take 'em up hot to meet Dad... We used to think it was marvellous to walk up there. We'd actually go where they all were in the cuddy to see them there with their pasties." Jack Michael and family.

"In my schooldays, you'd get, boys mostly, asking permission to go early at the dinner-time break to take their father's dinner, usually a pasty. Was a regular thing, I can remember walking the best part of a mile, anyway to and from, come home, and have your own dinner, and walk back to school again!" Tom Westlake

"It was a tough life as a clay worker. Hard work. Back then they knew what a hard day's work was." Thelma Cann

'Winning the clay' is the term used to describe the process by which clay is extracted.

Since it's discovery in Cornwall, the process of extracting clay has remained the same for over 260 years. Today, what would have essentially been done by the hands of large teams of men, is carried out by fewer workers and very large pieces of equipment.

Before any clay can be extracted from the earth, workers have to remove what is known as the 'overburden' or 'overburthen', a 1m to 20m layer of top soil and subsoil that lies on top of the clay bed.

During the 19th century the overburden would have been removed with pickaxes and shovels. Workers, under the supervision of shift captains (or cap'ns), would start at 5am (having walked to work) and finished around midday (that was the 'fore noon' shift). Other afternoon and night shifts made clay extraction a 24 hour operation and it still is!

At some time or another, every clay pit in Cornwall would have had a shift captain. During peak production ECLP employed over 100 shift captains across the pits of Devon and Cornwall. Some trained on the job and others came from Camborne School of Mines.

The shift cap'n, a phrase which replaced the term shift boss, was the man who sorted and took charge of the shifts, checked the equipment, logged the men's hours, organised the wages and dished out the discipline.

"Things went on in the pits and the shift cap'n was there to ensure things didn't!" Ivor Bowditch

All the old pit workers can remember a captain or two, he was the boss and no two ways about it. Some were revered for their hardness, others for their humanity.

"If the cap'n had had enough you were finished"

"Cap'n Dick was very good. Now see, if you wanted to have a day off sick, he wouldn't exactly check you. When he was loading clay or had something special on, he'd ask you to work on and he'd make your pay good but you had to work his time." Ray Neal

200 years ago, teams of pit workers could move anything up to 20 tons of rock before lunchtime. With spines of steel and hands like shovels they'd then cycle or walk home often labouring at a local farm in the afternoon or work on their own small holding.

Today, the overburden is broken by blasting the rock and then it's removed by large dumper trucks.

Imerys uses an average of 3,000 tons of explosives to break somewhere in the region of 3.5 million tons of rock every single year (now that is hardcore!)

Once the overburden is removed, the granite rock face reveals the layers and layers of clay-bearing ground. At this stage the decomposed white feldspar is still mixed with mica and quartz and the most effective way of separating out the clay is to wash it!

In the early days, workers washed the clay by diverting a stream over the rock face. This would flush and separate the parts as men below broke the clay with 'dubbers', the slurry from which would then flow to the bottom of the pit.

Today the clay is washed by what's known as a 'monitor' – a giant hose pipe with a narrow nozzle which blasts the clay face with water.

The water hoses wash out the clay at a pressure of 300psi – that's about 3,000 gallons a minute, enough to knock over a Landrover (or blow a hole through you and me).

After being washed from the rock face, the clay is still a long way from being ready to ship to market. First it has to be 'liberated' from the slurry.

As the suspension of white clay, mica and quartz flows away from the rock face the larger and coarser materials, containing mica and quartz sands, settle and the clay particles float to the top.

What remains in the water flows to the 'sink' of the pit where it's lifted by giant centrifugal pumps to mechanical classifiers, which remove more of the coarse sand.

At this point in the process the thick, whitish, grey slurry is 90% china clay. This mixture is then pumped from the open-cast mines to large settling tanks at the top.

Once pumped from the pit, a sedimentation process removes all the smaller sized particles leaving only china clay behind.

Imerys has in the region of 160 miles worth of pipeline in operation, pumping the water and clay suspension throughout the various stages of its extraction. The pipelines move about 7,000 gallons a minute, that's about 60 tons of dry clay per hour!

Centuries ago, china clay slurry would have been passed through what was known as a 'drag' – a large rectangular pit walled with stone designed to separate out the really fine sand and mica from the clay.

The mica men or 'mikee men' would empty the fine sand out of the channels, which were cleared using drains. When the plugs on the drains were pulled, the waste sand would be discharged out into the local rivers.

Once the clay-refining process had taken place, the white slurry would flow into another tank where it would be allowed to settle and thicken and any wastewater allowed to drain away. The thick clay would then be moved into large sun pans to dry in the sunshine (they must have had proper summers back then!).

The clay would then be cut into blocks and sorted into various grades, the finest of which would be cleaned by the bal-maidens and then stored in giant clay dries.

Today the liquid clay, which is pumped straight from the pit, goes through a process of filtration to remove any remaining debris leaving a solid material, which is about 25% moisture. It's then passed through a thermal drier, powered by natural gas, producing a material that is 10% water – only now is the clay ready to be shipped to market.

The main by-products of the china clay extraction process are sand and mica.

The famous turquoise lakes and pools of Cornwall's clay area are given their bluey-green hue by the mica particles, left over from washing the clay.

The sand, which comes freshly washed, contains high levels of white quartz. When it's tipped, the sparkling clean sand gives the landscape the white peaks the area is so famous for.

Today, every year approaching 2 million tons of waste sand and rock are removed from the pits and sold to the secondary aggregate industry.

Crushed rock and sand from the clay pits of Cornwall helped to build the Olympic Village for London 2012.

Aggregate from the clay was used to build what was known as the Cornish Unit, an important form of housing for those made homeless by the bombings of the Second World War.

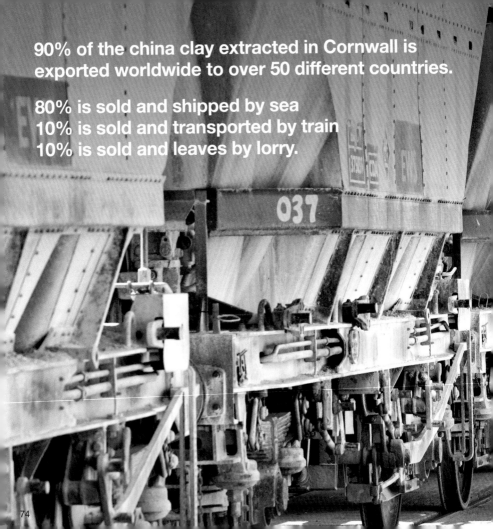

90% of the china clay extracted in Cornwall is exported worldwide to over 50 different countries.

80% is sold and shipped by sea
10% is sold and transported by train
10% is sold and leaves by lorry.

Today, the clay train starts at Rocks in Bugle. From the giant storage sheds, china clay is lifted onto some 32 freight carriages which are pulled from the pits on the edge of St Austell to the port at Fowey.

In times gone by china clay would have also been shipped from Charlestown and Par.

Charlestown harbour, famous the world over for its square-sail fleet of sailing ships, is a small port which began as a fishing village called Polmear. The port was named after Charles Rashleigh – a local landowner who pioneered its design.

Even this comparatively tiny, little fishing port had worldwide significance because of the seafaring connections it had created through the shipping of Cornwall's clay. After the horse drawn carts had made their way down to Charlestown, clay was loaded and shipped across the globe.

Today, Charlestown is one of the finest remaining examples of a 19th century fishing harbour.

With 46 listed buildings it's hardly changed (perhaps that's why it's been featured in more TV dramas and Hollywood movies than anywhere else in Cornwall - credits include The Eagle Has Landed, The Onedin Line, Rebecca, Mansfield Park and Dr Who!)

Charlestown's iconic sailing ships are the only working square-sail fleet left in the world. Not only are they the stars of Charlestown harbour but they also star in over 50 different feature films and documentaries too.

The Shipwreck Centre, home to the largest underwater diving equipment collection in England, is the largest private collection of its kind in Europe. The exhibitions not only show a wide range of maritime history, but they also reflect village life in Charlestown and its role within the clay industry.

STERY

If you happen to be enjoying a quick drink at the Pier House Hotel or are soaking up the evening views from the harbour wall, you might be lucky enough to catch the gig rowing team launching their boats.

Charlestown Rowing Club began on 22nd May 1990 when 20 locals got together at the Rashleigh Arms and decided to start a gig rowing squad.

After raising £12,000 to pay for its first boat, Charlestown soon became one of the strongest clubs in Cornwall. Today it has over 100 members and is very active within the community, helping to organise regatta week, the village carnival and their famous Boxing Day swim!

Six-oared wooden pilot gig boats are unique to Cornwall and the Isles of Scilly. They date back to the late 1790s when they were used to row pilots out to the large square-riggers who traded from and around the Cornish coast. Pilots were local seafarers who helped large ships navigate to port.

The oldest gig boat competing today belongs to Newquay Gig club. Built in 1838, the 32ft boat _Treffry_ is named after the local mineral company and civil engineer, who inherited his family estate at Place in Fowey.

Joseph Treffry, a civil engineer from Devon, was responsible for developing the first commercial minerals quay in Fowey and the port at Par Harbour.

Having taken control of Fowey Consols in 1822, the most productive group of mines in Cornwall, Treffry needed a more economic way to ship tin. The minimal facilities and narrow streets made transporting clay to and from Fowey docks a costly and labour intensive process, which inspired Treffry to draw up plans for a new port in Par.

In 1829 Treffry completed a 12,000ft breakwater. By 1833 he had finished the port. The new harbour could handle 50 vessels each able to carry up to 200 tons of clay or tin. By 1858 Par Docks was handling 15,000 tons of white clay every year.

Par Harbour has been non-operational since 2007 but the vast warehouses are still home to Imerys' European Milling Centre. In the next few years Par Docks is set to become 'one of the best marinas in the UK' as part of the Eco Town developments planned by Imerys and Orascom (more about that later).

Par, Cornish for 'Porth', was once a tiny coastal village beneath the cliff-face on the edge of the River Par, overlooking St Austell Bay.

What originally began as a series of small seaside cottages is now a thriving community with over 1,400 inhabitants, some great local pubs, a cracking fish and chip shop, Pearns of Par (who make some of the largest pasties on the planet) and not forgetting the mid Cornwall athletics track (much needed to burn off all those calories).

Par Beach or 'Parbados' or 'The Parhamas' as it's lovingly nicknamed, is a well-known spot for families, dog-walkers, birdwatchers and kite-surfers on the south coast of Cornwall.

The beach, which is wide and shallow with sandy dunes, backs onto a local nature reserve and is overlooked by the Gribbin Lighthouse. The area has been a popular sunbathing and holiday spot since the 1900s.

Take a short walk in the easterly direction along the South West Coast Path from Par and you'll reach Polkerris or 'Pollkerys', Cornish for 'fortified pool'.

Polkerris is a sandy cove home, to the Polkerris Beach Company, who operate the watersports school, Sams on the Beach, a popular pizzeria operating from the old lifeboat station and the Rashleigh Inn. (In short it's a top spot to grab a bite to eat or a hot drink before getting back in your boat or back on your feet).

The village, once famous for its lifeboat station built in 1859, is a tiny harbour owned by the Rashleigh family who reside at their family home Menabilly – just up the road. The local pub is named after them.

Between 1943 and 1969, Menabilly was the home of Daphne du Maurier. The house was the inspiration for Manderley in her famous novel *Rebecca*, which was also set in woodland and hidden from view from the sea.

Whilst the house is still a private family home, two of the cottages are available as holiday lets, one being quite literally a stone's throw from the shore at Polridmouth Beach.

Walk a few more miles east and you'll arrive in Fowey, the only port in Cornwall exporting china clay today.

Fowey (pronounced the same way as joy but with an F!) **is named after the River Fowey. The estuary inspired Kenneth Grahame, who married in the town, to write** *Wind in the Willows* (the Fowey Hall Hotel being Toad Hall of course).

The mouth of the harbour, the beginning or end of the famous Saint's Way (depending on which way you walk it) lies between St Catherine's Castle to the west, built by Henry VIII, and Polruan Headland to the east.

Fowey, the famous home of Sir Arthur Quiller Couch, Daphne du Maurier and more recently Dawn French, has been shipping china clay from its estuary port since the 1800s.

Fowey is a deep-water harbour, which allows it to handle large clay ships. Up until the late 1980s, Fowey was one of Britain's largest exporting ports in terms of tonnage handled.

In 1989, over 1.8 million tons of china clay were shipped through the port. Today it moves 600,000 to 700,000 tons each year, that's about 200 ships worth.

More recently Fowey has become a popular port for large cruise liners, a convenient stop off for those travelling by sea who want to find out more about the life and works of Daphne du Maurier or visit the Eden Project!

The famous Daphne du Maurier Festival draws people from all over the world and Fowey Royal Regatta is a top spot for the southwest's sailing community and Britain's fastest aircraft team – the Red Arrows.

The Red Arrows have been performing at Fowey Regatta since 1977. In 2002 the committee celebrated the 25th anniversary of the Red Arrows coming to Fowey. That year determined not to disappoint the crowds, a pilot went through the entire display without any instrumentation – doing the whole show at 400mph entirely from memory!

The incredibly popular event engages the whole community and has a long and proud history with the royals having attracted visits from Queen Victoria, Prince Albert and Queen Elizabeth II.

The week-long festivities are organised and marshalled entirely by local volunteers, the event is funded by donations and costs over £30,000 and is enjoyed by thousands.

From Fowey, Cornwall's white gold heads along the English Channel to the paper mills of Scandinavia and south on the Atlantic to the ceramics industries of the Mediterranean and North Africa.

The largest use of china clay is in the production of paper – it is also used as a coating to create the glossy look on magazine covers. Yes you'll find it in ceramics – but don't forget how big that business is. We're not just talking cups, plates and bowls, we're talking chamber pots, toilets too and all manner of bathroom sanitary ware.

And while we're in the bathroom – you'll find kaolin in toothpaste.
And as you powder your face – you'll find it there too – it's used in face packs and all manner of cosmetics.
If that hasn't shed enough light on the matter – you'll find china clay as the light diffusing material in white incandescent light bulbs.
It's used in paint manufacture (and that's no whitewash!).
It's used in rubber manufacture (how tyring!).
In some parts of the world it's used in the production of smoking pipes (stick that in your pipe and smoke it!).
In Nepal they use it to whitewash their homes.

In organic farming a light spray of kaolin over some crops can ward off insect damage and if you spray it gently throughout an orchard, it stops the sun scalding the fruits' skin (sun cream for apples). Kaolin is also used to treat an upset stomach and diarrhoea – some cultures eat it to suppress hunger (nice).

"There was a time when it was easier to name the products china clay didn't go into rather than those that it did."

Des Carter, the last shift cap'n at Stannon Pit.

As more uses for china clay were discovered, more workers were needed to extract it. Just like the mining communities further west, in the St Austell area wherever there was a white hole in the ground, there was a Cornishman at the bottom of it. Very soon villages grew around the edges of pits, providing homes for the workers.

From the late 1800s, the Hensbarrow uplands, just north of St Austell, became the heart of Cornwall's china clay country. Villages such as Treviscoe, Bugle, Foxhole, Stenalees, Nanpean, St Dennis and St Stephen-in-Brannel were at the very centre of the industry.

Between 1800 and 1850, the population of St Austell and the surrounding area more than doubled. Cornwall's white gold was fast becoming the economic cornerstone of the area.

Hamlets became villages and existing villages grew into fiercely independent strongholds with their own schools, shops, churches and social clubs.

The churches provided a place for biblical guidance and the social clubs provided entertainment, with both institutions giving birth to the vast number of bands and choirs the area is famous for.

As the number of villages grew, so did the number of religious and community happenings.

The events calendar in clay country was soon to be crammed with harvest festivals, special Saint's days, tea treats and carnival parades.

Not to mention the competitions and crownings of village carnival queens and performances from local or visiting bands, choirs and pantomime groups.

Large events like the Summercourt Fair, the West of England Bandsmen's Festival and village feast weeks, gave villagers the opportunity to socialise and compete against each other. This was either through carnival queen parading, musical performance or sheer brute force. Local men could flex their muscles in rivalry during a good old tug-of-war or compete in wrestling.

The Summercourt Fair, held in the parish of St Enoder, on the northern fringes of clay country, is over 750 years old.

Cornwall Council have documents dating the Charter Fair back to 1234. Traditionally it was held on the 14th September every year, today it is still the largest event of its kind in Cornwall and the oldest surviving fair in Great Britain.

"Summercourt, used to love it. Both sides of the street were full of stalls. My cousin was a builder and whenever we had an outing he'd tie benches to the back of his truck and we'd all travel down to the fair sitting on those seats, strapped to his works vehicle. You couldn't do it now." Jennifer Pursall

"We used to have the day off for Summercourt. Once a year they'd run a double-decker bus there and we'd run down to the edge of the village to see it. We'd never seen one before."

"When it was feast week, we used to go to St Stephen for the wrestling... we had some very good times and that's where I picked my husband up.

Well, we missed the bus and we had to walk home and when I got home I was streaming wet.

I courted for five year and got married when I was 25."

Long before the invention of the wireless and almost six decades before Glastonbury, the first West of England Bandsmen's Festival took place at Peniel, in aptly named Bugle on Saturday 14th September, 1912.

A century ago, the festival was organised entirely by volunteers (and still is) as an attempt to help raise funds to build the Workingmen's Club still standing in the village today. Each committee member put up a sovereign, which was paid into the local bank to guarantee the prize money.

An outstanding 6,000 people attended the event to hear 10 bands from Devon and Cornwall, the first to compete for those precious gold sovereigns. The winners were Camborne Town in Class A and Foxhole Temperance in Class B.

The competition was such a success that it was inevitable it would become a regular event. Since then, with the exception of 1933 and the war years, the festival has been held in Bugle and now takes place at Mollinis Park.

Today, the West of England Bandsmen's Festival is the only remaining open-air bandsmen's competition in Great Britain.

The West of England Bandsmen's Festival starts 45 minutes before the contest with each of the bands parading down Bugle High Street (one of the most moving musical mornings you'll ever experience in mid-Cornwall).

During the parade, bands are marked on their deportment (the judge hides in a house en route). The rest of the time they are rated on their musical performance, with each band playing the same pieces of music.

In 2012, the West of England Bandsmen's Festival celebrated its centenary, having held 88 competitions since it began.

Today it's the only brass band festival in the world where bands compete for a Royal Trophy, donated to the event in 1913 by the Prince of Wales.

At the very end of the day the winners of the Royal Trophy proudly perform in 'The Square', just outside the Bugle Inn.

As the last band plays, crowds gather, the traffic comes to a standstill and is held back by the police. It's an incredibly special moment.

"For any band in Cornwall, playing in 'The Square' is like playing at the Royal Albert Hall... When our band won, we played in the square and I couldn't believe it, I played with tears streaming down my face." Helen Farmer

Twas contest day in Bugle,
The greatest day of the year
And people came from everywhere
Their favourite bands to hear

The weather was unfavourable
And somewhat marred the day
But thousands stood around that stand
To hear the bandsmen play.

W.T. Hawkey 1920

"We'd be wet to our skin, with music pegged to the stands, but we'd still get up and play. Our family is banding. My grandad, my uncle, the kids and me. It's the teamwork and after the contest it's a good excuse for a knee's up." Tracy Bristow

In the clay, bandsmenship was a family tradition with generations and neighbours teaching each other. It still remains the same with girls and boys as young as seven playing today.

Brass and silver bands could be found in St Dennis, Penwithick, Stenalees, Bugle, Indian Queens, Sticker, Foxhole, Mountcharles and St Austell. Nanpean was known for its fife and drum troupe.

More than half of these groups still play today punching well above their weight on the national scene. Many tour the country in regular competitions, which have included events at Alexandra Palace and the Royal Albert Hall.

With most bands originating during the late 1700s and mid-1800s, Cornwall's clay country created some of the first and finest bands in Great Britain. They are an important part of the area's heritage.

Today, many actively encourage young membership offering free lessons on Saturdays or weekday evenings and free instrument hire.

In the tradition of many Methodist and mining communities and similar to those of Wales and northern England, the china clay area was once a choral capital of Cornwall.

Most famously in 1955, Treviscoe Male Voice Choir won a place to compete in the International Eisteddfod, Llangollen, Wales, a musical competition attracting choirs from all over the world.

After beating groups from other parts of England, Wales, Germany, Yugoslavia and the USA, the Treviscoe men came home as the British Champions, second only to the Italian choir, which included the young Luciano Pavarotti!

In 1956, they won!

Whilst the Treviscoe Choir no longer exists, the tradition of male voices from the clay is very much upheld by the tender tones of the Imerys Mid-Cornwall Male Choir, directed by Barry Hawken.

Mixed community choirs in the area include the Champagne Ladies, the Imerys Singers, the St Austell Choral Society and the Eden Choir, all of whom continue to keep the tradition of coming together in song alive in the clay today.

Drive through most clay villages during the summer months and you'll be amazed by the number of hand-made signs and banners promoting the season's wealth of carnivals, fetes, shows and gymkhanas.

Choose to attend one of these colourful village carnivals and you'll be as equally bowled over by the wealth of creativity that can come from a cardboard box, a packet of face paints, a pair of tights, a stapler and a crew of Young Farmers with a fancy dress theme!

Cornwall's clay villages have a long-standing carnival and carnival queen tradition. It was a way for villages to show off their carnival queens and the events that took place allowed villagers to compete in a fun and tongue-in-cheek manner. The tradition of carnival was also a way to raise vital funds for community resources, many of the social clubs and recreation fields standing today are testament to the success and popularity of this tradition.

"Well, there was no television in my day so everyone took part. The carnival parade was how the villages showed off their carnival queens. I was the first-ever fairy queen where I lived and we had the attendants, then the queens.

We'd all be voted for by the public in a village contest beforehand. Then we'd be given some money for our outfit and then it was the carnival parade. It was such a special day. Each village had its own event and if you weren't actually dressed up or on the wagons, you'd be out on the streets watching.

The most special thing was getting up early to dress the wagons. The company would drop them off early and by the time they were finished they looked wonderful, covered in hydrangeas - beautiful they were." Jennifer Pursall

"It was the sound that put hairs on the back of my neck. As the parade pulled off you'd hear the band, the thud of the horses big hooves on the road and the jingling of all the harnesses - it was so exciting - really special." Kath Goodman

Before the beginning of the Second World War, every August bank holiday, Jack Couch's field in the centre of Par was centre stage for one of the area's largest carnivals. The event was so popular that extra trains were timetabled to carry visitors from Plymouth.

Just up the road, in the neighbouring village of Biscovey, 2012 saw the centenary of May Day celebrations with the latest carnival queen receiving a commemoration letter from her Majesty the Queen.

The crowning of the Biscovey carnival queen is believed to be the oldest carnival queen celebration of its kind on record.

In Rescorla, a small village in the parish of Treverbyn, the oldest community festival involves 'tea treats and snail creeps'.

Alongside the villages of Molinnis, Roche, Withiel and St Wenn, the folk of Rescorla used to participate in a strange little parading custom known as the Snail Creep.

In the Snail Creep Dance the villagers are led by a band and a pair of dancers holding branches which represent the eyestalks of a snail. The large procession then moves up the street.

At the top of the village everyone forms a circle and then spirals in and out of it, just like the swirls on a snail's shell. In the old days the dance was accompanied by the Mollinis Fife and Drum group, who last performed in the village 60 years ago.

In 2008, volunteers from Rescorla reinvigorated their village festival and re-enacted the Snail Creep – for the first time in more than six decades.

The largest community event to appear on the clay country calendar belongs to the St Austell Torchlight Carnival, which has lit up local streets since November 2008.

The event begins at John Keay House and is sponsored by a wealth of local businesses with local organisations and charities fitting out their carnival floats to compete for prizes.

The stars of the show are created by local schoolchildren, who work with community artists to create giant withie and paper sculptures, which parade through the town.

Another wintertime treat is a trip to see one of the local pantomime groups treading the boards in their local community centre.

Pantomime groups were, and still are, an important part of the culture of Cornwall's clay. With low wages and limited transport, leisure time was spent very much in the locality so most of the clay villages had their own theatrical group.

Because the groups encouraged performers of all ages, sexes and abilities, they strengthened the inter-generational and social bonds in each area and offered a creative outlet for local talent, performers, closet costume designers and directors alike.

With a history that dates back to 1943, St Stephen's Pantomime Group is the oldest in the area.

"It was started by Harold Lander who owned the local radio shop and began as a series of concerts. This soon grew into pantomime performances. I remember the first costumes were made of dyed muslin. There were a good 30 people in the cast, it took over the whole village and then we toured some of the villages, Nanpean and Laddock."
Margaret Northey

Other pantomime groups still exist in St Dennis, Trewoon, Roche, St Austell, Indian Queens and St Blazey – needless to say the area has plenty of local characters!

Pull up next to the China Café at the junction of Trinity Street and Truro Road, St Austell, you'll see a very special mural celebrating some of the most notable real life characters in the area. It was designed and painted by Janet Shearer, a world-renowned trompe l'oeil artist, who has lived locally since 1976.

Trompe l'oeil, pronounced 'tromp loy' is French for 'trick the eye'. The term describes a style of painting where the artist creates an illusion of space by creating an apparently three dimension image on a wall making the onlooker believe that the image is not flat and that space exists where it really isn't.

The mural in St Austell is filled with local characters including: Clay country-born writer and poet Jack Clemo; Tregonissey-born historian A L Rowse; founder of the St Austell Brewery, Sir Walter Hicks; St Austell-born Bishop John Colenso, the first Anglican Bishop of Natal, South Africa; Luxulyan-born architect of the 19th century Silvanus Trevail; Beatrice Rogers the first-ever female deaconess in the Methodist church and of course William Cookworthy who discovered china clay. And don't forget Daphne du Maurier on the balcony!

Famous local folk from the present include St Austell-born actor John Nettles; St Austell-born England goalkeeper Nigel Martyn; former England rugby player Richard Sharp and British athletics champion Jemma Simpson. (Oh, and the very handsome waiter is photographer James Ram, many of whose pictures are in this book.)

"Many of the characters seated at the back row of tables are personal friends and family, except for Jenson Button, who was added at the request of my assistant - the waitress on the left who thought he was gorgeous! I made him look admiringly at her forever, in spite of the fact that he was seated at a table with my daughter, who also thought he was gorgeous. The two dogs are our family pets." Janet Shearer

There was a time, not so long ago, when every clay village would have had its own football team and a few had teams for cricket and bowls.

Tug of war was a popular team event during Feast Week, as was wrestling and the village of St Columb was famous for it's Shrove Tuesday game of hurling.

No matter what was happening on the sporting or social calendar in the village - Sunday was 'chapel' or church.

"In times gone by the whole of Clay Country village life revolved around either the church or the chapel, as far as I can remember, never the two together.

Not only did they care for the soul, but provided virtually the only entertainment. The Sunday School Anniversary, with every little girl dressed not only in a very posh frock, but also a flower-bedecked straw hat; was closely followed by the tea-treat. There were races to be run, the band to be listened to and huge "tea-treat" saffron buns washed down with "sugary" tea poured from gigantic jugs.

It paid to go to Sunday School! All the local talent appeared in much-enjoyed concerts; singers, players of the "musical saw" and the performers of funny "sketches"

Also high on the village scene were the Temperance Societies, whose members had all foresworn alcohol: although I've heard that more than one Rechabite gentleman had been seen emerging from a far-flung hostelry.

Happily, we now have "Churches Together" where the clergy preach in each other's churches, joining together in helping the community; and village life is so much richer for it."

Clarice Westlake

"I sang in the choir. On anniversary day one year I wanted a new bag. I told my father I wouldn't sing unless he got me one. He did you know and I remember singing in the choir while clutching the strap of my new bag.

On Sunday school anniversary day we'd all get a new dress and the chapel would be packed. At Trethosa every nook and cranny was taken up with chairs for people.

Mr West always brought us roses that day and everyone's family members came home from wherever they were for the service. Different chapel Sunday schools had different anniversary days and we'd always have a tea treat afterwards.

We'd sit outside to have our tea-treat. Tea with sugar, saffron buns, one of the bands might come down, and there would be sack races in the fields. Treviscoe even had their own flora dance." Jennifer Pursall

Of the 535,300 folk living in Cornwall, the clay area, with all of its contours and characters, is home to just over 100,000 inhabitants – making it the largest conurbation in the county.

The Clay Country Local Action Area covers 11 parishes including St Enoder, St Dennis, Roche, Luxulyan, Lanlivery, Lostwithiel, St Stephen-in-Brannel, St Mewan, Treverbyn, St Blaise and Tywardreath.

Each of the clay villages, which grew around their own clay pit, have their own character and characters, their own church or preaching pit, their own special sporting team, their own band and their own entertainment troop of either singers or actors. (Not to mention the many scout and guide troupes, Young Farmers Clubs, Gardening Societies and Women's Institutes groups.

The village of Bugle, in the parish of Treverbyn, was founded in the 1840s and named after its coaching house, whose sign depicted a coaching horn.

The settlement grew after the construction of a turnpike road and the Par to Bugle railway line in 1842. Today, the population of Bugle and nearby Stenalees is over 2,500 people.

The Bugle Silver Band has been playing since 1868 and the village is famous for its bandsmen's festival, which began in 1912.

For most of us, Bugle is one of those villages that people pass through. It's on the main drag between the A30 and St Austell so not somewhere people stop. But... next time you pass, see if you can spot the planted shopping trolley – just one of the Bugle Green Space ideas working to create greener and more open spaces in the village.

The Bugle Green Space community group was started in 2008 by a crew of enthusiastic locals who wanted to make Bugle a greener place to live.

Now, with the assistance of over 50 volunteers they run regular litter picks, picnics in their park, they encourage villagers to share each others' gardens and are campaigning for their own orchard. Their project was so successful and infectious that it has inspired nearby villages like Treverbyn to do the same thing.

Treverbyn parish, formed in 1847, includes the villages of Treverbyn, Stenalees, Penwithick, Bugle, Bowling Green, Resugga Green, Kerrow Moor, Carthew, Ruddlemoor, Scredda and parts of Trethurgy.

The Treverbyn area is home to Carn Grey, a granite outcrop with a little quarry, which can be accessed via the clay trails above St Austell. It's well worth the walk and it's a top spot for views out over St Austell Bay.

In Penwithick you can't miss the famous giant skytip at Carluddon and just down the road in Ruddlemoor, you'll find Wheal Martyn – the only China Clay Museum in Great Britain!

If you take the clay trail above Carclaze you'll get a great view of Baal Pit, famous for being used in the 1971 BBC *Doctor Who* series with John Pertwee. The lunar landscape was filmed as the backdrop for the planet Uxarieus.

On the edge of Goss Moor, home to the local springs that create the headwaters of the River Fal, the village and parish of Roche is most famous for its rock (and if you hadn't guessed it Roche is French for Rock).

The rocky outcrop rises 20 metres out of the ground. It is of great interest to geologists because it's a very rare example of fully tourmalinised granite, which was granted SSSI status in 1991.

On the top of the rock stands the ruined St Michael's chapel, which, built entirely out of large granite blocks, cleverly incorporates Roche Rock into its architecture.

The church is two storeys high with a lower room believed to have been lived in by a hermit. His daughter fed him water through a hole in the rocks, known as Gonetta's well.

Nobody really knows why the church is there, some believe it would have stood as a beacon to guide travellers across the moor, others believe it was built to imitate the pilgrimage place of St Michael's Mount, West Cornwall. (We love it!)

It's well worth a visit, some organisations will even arrange for you to climb the rock, a ramble around it is just as enjoyable especially if you stop off at Roche's Rest and Play Café, for a cuppa and some cake afterwards.

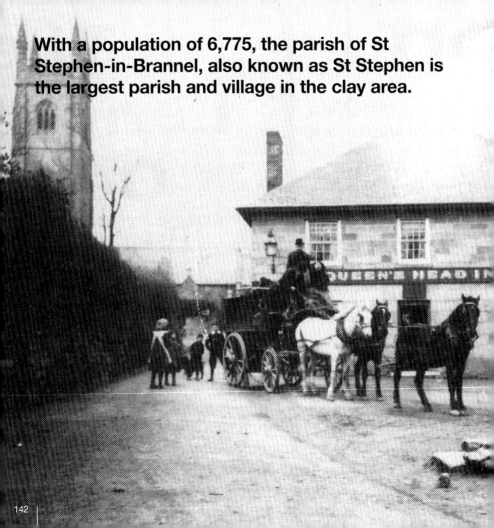

With a population of 6,775, the parish of St Stephen-in-Brannel, also known as St Stephen is the largest parish and village in the clay area.

St Stephen's parish council looks after the villages of Coombe, Foxhole, High Street, Lanjeth, Nanpean, Treviscoe and Whitemoor.

St Stephen is the only village in clay country to have a gold postbox, marking the Olympic medal achievements of Jonathan Fox, Paralympian swimmer and former pupil at Brannel School, who grew up the village.

The first Brannel School, for 11 to 16-year-olds, opened in 1961, then in September 2011, over half a century later, a brand new school opened – one of the most modern senior school buildings in Cornwall. The school was designed and developed with the help of its pupils (it's fab and lots of exciting community events have been happening in the school's Bell Theatre).

Nearby South Terras Mine, between St Stephen and Grampound, is famous for its production of radium and uranium, used in Marie Curie's research, which went on to develop radiotherapy for cancer patients.

When Kneehigh Theatre Company performed *Hell's Mouth*, Nick Darke's version of the Greek Play *Antigone*, at Longstone Pit, near Nanpean, the entire site became a theatre.

It was initially the only theatrical production in the world to be held within a china clay pit with stars that included local dirt-bikers, who were cast as Samurai stunt riders.

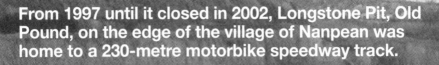

From 1997 until it closed in 2002, Longstone Pit, Old Pound, on the edge of the village of Nanpean was home to a 230-metre motorbike speedway track.

The Clay Country Moto Parc, which author Robert Bamford and track announcer Dave Stallworthy describe in their book *Clay Country Speedway*, was known as 'a remarkable track in a vast disused china clay pit with a wonderful lunar landscape setting... the most exciting circuit in British Speedway'.

Mid-Cornwall has had a long history with motorcross bike racing and the sport of speedway. St Austell had its first custom-built track at the Cornish Stadium, Par Moor. At a time when the only local entertainment was a trip to the Odeon cinema or a football match at St Blazey, Tuesday nights at the speedway track were the talk of the county.

"When it was floodlit at night, there was nowhere else like it in the world." Chris Varcoe

Jeremy Jackson, author of *St Austell Speedway*, reminisced that on Tuesday evenings 'residents of Grampound and Probus would regularly sit in their front gardens... just to catch the noise and spectacle of the traffic heading for Par Moor, with maybe a blue and white scarf trailing out of the window.'

"I can remember hearing the sound of the bikes in my back garden." Becky James

The first speedway competition at Par Moor took place on 14th June 1949. It was enjoyed by crowds of over 12,000 people. During the next four decades the track, which cost £10,000 and took two years to build, welcomed record crowds of up to 18,000. People travelled from all over the world to see the world champions of speedway race round the 360m track at Par.

The village of Whitemoor is home to the only half preaching pit in the world (Indian Queens has got a whole one!).

Indian Queens belongs to the parish of St Enoder which has a population of 4,500. It's the most northerly of the clay country parishes home to Fraddon, St Columb Road, Summercourt and Indian Queens.

The Indian Queens Pit was built inside a disused open mine. Local landowner Henry Rowse allowed the pit to be constructed after a request by local Wesleyans who wanted to create a replica of the famous Gwennap Pit.

The now scheduled monument was opened in 1850 by the local preacher, Captain Elvis of Retew. Within a decade the pit was used for weddings, anniversaries and often featured performances by the Indian Queens town band. When Mr Rowse's son wanted to sell the land a group of volunteers formed a consortium to save the pit and continued to use it for local events until 1970.

Over the next six years, the pit became overgrown until local man Mr Lloyd Truscott restored the site and updated its construction. It was officially reopened in 1978.

Today this wonderful spot, just tucked behind a housing estate on Barn Lane, is now used as a local theatre with performances by the town band and touring theatre companies. Fund-raising has enabled a new visitor's centre to be built just next door.

Built on a Bronze Age hill fort, St Dennis village is almost an island. It's the highest village in the clay.

With most of the local houses and cottages sitting 190m above sea level, the village retains much of its ancient charm. The wonderful grass-covered granite hedges which enclose small fields are just one of the age-old and endearing features of the settlement.

The St Dennis Band, which is believed to date back to 1838, has a history of competing on the world stage and in 2009 achieved championship status. They've won the Royal Trophy at the Bugle Bandsmen's Festival no less than 29 times!

In the last few years the village of St Dennis has hit the local and national headlines for its fight against plans for the Cornwall Energy Recovery Centre, an incinerator development where a huge proportion of Cornwall's waste will be burned instead of being dug into landfill.

The £117-150 million incinerator, with a chimney stack of over 120m, just 500m from the village, has been designed to burn over 240,000 tons of waste every year for the next thirty years.

The incinerator is expected to generate an annual 16 megawatts of electricity as well as 55,000 tons of bottom ash, 6,000 tons of highly toxic fly ash, and an extra 170,000 tons of CO_2 emissions.

Justifiably, locals have had many fears and reservations about the project; anxieties about their health being the highest, not to mention the dangers of the increased number of vehicles on quiet local roads as well as the implications of the toxic fumes on local farmland, farm animals and flora and fauna.

In November 2005, a group of passionate locals formed The St Dennis Incinerator Group (STIG) and for the last 7 years have campaigned valiantly against the large-scale development. Their fight, which has taken the incinerator plans and consultation process to the High Court and the Court of Appeal, has taken many twists and turns and been an exhausting and emotional ordeal for the village.

After a public enquiry at the Court of Appeal, in March 2012, Eric Pickles, Secretary of State, granted the project planning permission.

As we launched this book the **Cornwall Waste Forum** (St Dennis Branch) is publishing the results of an analysis of alternatives to the incinerator, anticipated to save Cornwall up to £9m a year. Only time will tell which choice Cornwall takes, and what will be the implications of that choice.

The threat of an incinerator is not the first time families or villages in Cornwall's clay have been under threat.

Centuries ago clay worker's jobs were far from secure and the work itself was fraught with physical risks. Over the years numerous homes and communities have vanished under the mountainous waste tips created from winning white clay.

The resilience of the people of the clay has been cultivated through the many challenges faced by clay working families and then handed down through each generation.

While the scattered villages and lunar landscape of the clay-land may appear desolate to outsiders they are not so to those who live there. The bonds which have built these settlements are tight, forming robust and powerful strongholds. Even today, each clay village maintains its unique identity. The connectedness, combined efforts and teamworking skills of the villagers sustain their many customs and give them the might to fight even the toughest of obstacles.

The largest new development proposed for Cornwall's clay is being managed by Eco-Bos. A company with a vision to positively transform 700 hectares of Imerys' owned former industrial land into several sustainable communities. The scheme, which is yet to be granted planning permission, has a long-term aim to create up to 5,500 new homes over the next 20 years. New developments will take place in the Baal and West Carclaze area, Blackpool, Goonbarrow, Drinnick and Nanpean. Par Docks will see a new marina.

As new communities are planned for disused pits and tips on ex-clayworking land, it's worth remembering that many villages have disappeared to make way for the industry's expansion.

The villages which have disappeared include Hornick, buried under Blackpool Tip; Halviggan, a hamlet of some 57 houses which lies beneath Blackpool Pit; and Karslake, now the largest China Clay Quarry complex in the world, which used to be home to 24 houses.

In the Fal Valley, Melador village, complete with its school, was swallowed up by developments at Melbur Pit.

And the most recent village to go, Retew, a settlement of 24 homes, vanished under tips and pits during the expansion of Wheal Remfry during the 1960s.

All of Retew's residents were re-housed by The English China Clay Company, but road signs still exist just off the A30, as if the village was still there.

In 2005, when poet Jack Clemo's cottage was demolished in order to make way for clay company laboratories, the local community was in uproar.

Jack Clemo, Cornish Bard, crowned poet of clay country and son of a clay-kiln worker was born in March 1916 at Goonamarris.

He lived and worked there for most of his literary life. From the age of five, Clemo began to go blind, just over twelve years later at the age of 18 he had lost most of his sight and was becoming hard of hearing.

Nevertheless, from the humble beginnings of writing regular letters to the local newspaper, Clemo's prose and poetry gained international recognition when he won a Festival of Britain prize in 1951.

Much of Clemo's work was inspired by his faith and the rugged landscape of Cornwall and the clay country.

Despite a local campaign to preserve the cottage, it too went for the clay. However, for now there is a small memorial room to Clemo's life and work in the Methodist chapel, just up from St Stephen at Trethosa.

Jack Clemo's portrait is on display at the National Gallery.

Like many small communities in the county, Cornwall's clay villages have their own language and local terms to describe things.

You'll often hear the words 'crib' used to describe a mid-morning snack, before dinner (which was at lunch time) and the world 'cuddy' is describes a clay workers shed or crib hut where they'd shelter and sit to eat their pasty.

When the pupils of Brannel School, St Stephen, did a survey of the many terms and words used in the local dialect, this is what they found:

If it's 'streamin out', it means it's raining and if it's 'skiffing' it means it's raining in the wind (and we sure get a lot of that down here).

If anyone tells you to look at the 'parish lantern' when it's 'dummaty' – they mean look at the moon at twilight. If anyone tells you to look out for the 'Mevagissey Hounds' – they mean the seagulls!

Clunkin' is a clay term for swallowing and if you're 'clunkin' like a toad' it means you're gulping (and probably quite loudly).

If you're 'filled like a wilkie' it means you're bloated (through either too many pasties or you're filled with pride).

If you're 'gapin' you are yawning.

If you've 'got the rats' it means you're in a bad mood.

If you're told you're a 'shiner' it means you're good looking.

If you're 'fitty wisht' it means you're really ill.

If you're in a 'fouch' you're in a muddle.

If you're 'mazed as a curly' you're as confused as a curlew.

If you're 'rampin' it means you're angry.

If you're 'diggin like a want' it means you're working really hard.

If you're clicky (like me), it means you're left-handed!

If you're a bit 'girdy' it means you're dirty.

To have a 'geek' means to take a look, but if you're 'glazing' it means you're staring.

And if you're 'zamzoddled' it means you burned or dried out in the oven!

The language of the clay not only speaks through the words of the locals but it also communicates through the tuneful lilts in their voices. But also, just look at all the wonderful words used across all the different pits and place names.

Littlejohns, Dorothy, **Dubbers**, Treviscoe

Kernick, Trethosa, Longstone, Noppies

Rosevallen, **Carloggas**, Foxhole, Hornick

Wheal Louisa, Rosemellyn, Halviggan

Blackpool, Virginia, Burgotha, Melbur, Meledor

Wheal Henry, **Rocks**, Rosevear, Wheal Anna

Goonbarrows, Trethowel, Great Bean

New Caudledown, **Bluebarrow**, Carbean

Gunheath, Wheal Martyn, **Greensplat**

Carrancarrow, **Great Longstone**

West Gunheath, Lower Ninestones, High

Ninestones, **Singlerose, Lansalson,** Great

Halwyn, Anchor, Fal Valley, Hendra **Halle**

Bloomdale, Penhale, Ruddle West Carclaze, Great Treverbyn, Carclaze Carvear, Bodelva, Wheal Remfry, Goonvean, Wheal Frederick, Gothers Callivet, Kerrow Moor, Benallack, Wheal Metallack, South Fraddon, Great Treviscoe Central Treviscoe, Carpalla, Gonnamarres Rostowrack, Trelavour, Parkandillick, Higher Halviggan, Cocksbarrow Forest, Hensbarrow, Ruddle Common, Ventrough, Trethurgy, Alsamor, North Goonbarrow, Wheal Prosper, Imperial Goonbarrow, Criggan, Treskilling, Prideaux Trewhela, Lantern, Belowda and Methrose

St Austell, which has been affectionately nicknamed 'Snozzle' has over 26,000 inhabitants. It's the largest town in Cornwall.

St Austell gets its name from Saint Austol or Austolus, a sixth-century Breton Christian who settled in the area to sow the seeds of the Christian faith. The first recorded mention of the town comes from an account by Henry VIII who described it as a small village centred around a church.

12th-century Holy Trinity church, still standing today, was dedicated in 1259 by the Bishop of Exeter. The building was built from Elvan stone, a fine building rock quarried from Pentewan. Check out the gargoyles on the outside of the building (and can you spot the pelican?).

Although the area is mostly associated with clay, the wealth that built St Austell came from mining. St Austell was in the stannary of Blackmore and during the 1830s the area's mines were the largest sources of tin in Cornwall. At one time it was possible to walk from Boscoppa Farm to Crinnis without coming to the surface!

At current prices, Carclaze, Crinnis, Charlestown United, Wheal Eliza, which is under Tregrehan Gardens, and Polgooth mine would have each produced over 100 million pounds worth of tin in their life time.

Between the late 1500s and 1800s most of St Austell's local population were involved in tin mining. The demand for tin was so high that in 1580, Queen Elizabeth invited German miners to the area. Today's local family names of Lobb, Kessell, Sleeman, Stark and Waldron came from these settlers.

St Austel is home to local community radio station St Austell Bay Radio and the local newspaper the St Austell Voice. The town also boasts having the head offices of some of the oldest family businesses still operating in Cornwall.

Coodes of St Austell have been practicing solicitors in the town since 1747 and today it's one of the largest law firms in the county.

160-year-old St Austell Brewery is one of the oldest, still family run breweries in Great Britain. It's been brewing beer since 1851 when the business was begun by Sir Walter Hicks.

Hicks started out as a maltster supplying malt to inns and ale houses within the St Austell area. In 1863 he bought the Seven Stars pub, just next to the Red Bank at No. 1 East Hill. The pub is believed to be the place where he brewed and pulled his very first pint of beer.

In 1893 he opened the brewery, which still stands on Trevannion Road today, and by 1912 the brewery had doubled its output and was sourcing the 'liquor' for the beer from a local stream, known as 'The Brake'.

Today, after several expansions and being the first-ever business in St Austell to have a telephone, the brewery continues to make Tribute, the region's most popular beer, and many more ales and brews.

The most modern architectural features in St Austell are White River Place, a brand new shopping centre, named after the nearby St Austell stream; and the White River Cinema, the county's newest picture house.

The £75 million development took seven years to build and opened in October 2009 (just as the country fell into recession and high-street giant Woolworth's went into liquidation).

Needless to say, with no less than four supermarkets on the edge of town, and another two being planned for as part of further out-of-town retail developments, it's no surprise that times have been hard for White River and St Austell as a whole.

Like many once-thriving market towns across Great Britain, despite huge efforts to keep sole-trader shops open whilst encouraging high-street chains, many of the units have remained empty and an uncomfortably large percentage of the town's oldest independent traders have closed.

In July 2012, White River Place was sold to retailer developers Ellandi. Hopes are high that the new owner can encourage new business so that the area can continue to develop as a tourist and shopping destination and grow a much-needed nighttime economy.

At 35m high and 220m long, the stone viaduct which links St Austell by rail to the rest of Cornwall was opened in 1899. The construction, which was first made of wood, is built on a curve. It's one of 42 viaducts built in Cornwall during the 1800s

St Austell's Grade II listed Market House, which opened in 1844, has been home to a market hall, fire station, police cells and picture house. When it was built it was believed to have the largest unsupported span of any roof in Britain! Today it's still open for trade and its history can be found on the walls all around the building – well worth a look.

Just up from Biddicks Court, you'll find The Old Press – a not-for-profit organisation and gallery dedicated to selling and showing the work of local artists. The Old Press building has been renovated and is a delightful spot to stop and enjoy local arts and crafts.

Other sites worth noting in the town include the Red Bank, built in 1898 and designed by famous architect Silvanus Trevail. The bricks were especially imported from Ruabon in North Wales.

Trevail also designed the houses on Moorland Terrace and more famously the Thin End, St Austell's favourite tea and cake shop.

St Austell began to emerge as a holiday destination after the arrival of the passenger railway in 1859.

By the 1950s beach huts and caravan parks had appeared at Par and Pentewan and St Austell was the only town in Cornwall where you could arrive by train and still pack your car!

The first large-scale tourist hotel to be built along what's become known as the Cornish Riviera, was the St Austell Bay Hotel now the Carlyon Bay Hotel, which opened in 1925.

During the 1930s and on the advice of Edward, Prince of Wales, a regular visitor to the area with his lover Mrs Simpson, the Cornish Riviera Club was developed down on the beach. The new seaside leisure complex offered open-air tennis courts, an Olympic-sized swimming pool and other sporting facilities.

The complex, which began as Cornish Leisure World and became the Cornwall Coliseum, was never entirely finished but is most fondly remembered in local memory for its roller discos, WOMAD festivals, and Gossips Nightclub.

During its heyday, before it had to compete with the nightspots of Newquay, the Cornwall Coliseum was the only venue in Cornwall to have a 2,000 person capacity. Today, its tattered remains are waiting to be redeveloped into a new beach-side resort, the first plans for which were proudly displayed at Selfridges in London.

The coarse, sandy beach at Carlyon Bay was formed from china clay waste, which washed down and gradually created a shoreline. It soon became a popular leisure spot and it sounds like the area will soon be regenerated and enjoyed again.

The many regeneration and land restoration projects, which have taken place in Cornwall's white country, have won national and international acclaim.

Quarrying for china clay has had a profound impact on the local landscape so huge investment has gone into restoring and reprofiling the Cornish Alps, as they are known locally.

In May 2008, The China Clay Woodland Project reached its completion. A staggering one million trees had been planted creating over 860 hectares of virgin woodland.

The land restoration project, funded by Objective One, Imerys and Natural England, took four years to complete and involved the planting of over 838 acres in the area. All of the planting took place on Imerys-owned land and was the largest woodland planting scheme in the entire country.

In fact, since the 1970s over 4,000 acres of heathland and woodland have been restored in the clay and 18km of trails have opened up.

Won't it be interesting to see what the landscape will look like in another 40 years. What will this enormous wooded wilderness attract in terms of new species and wildlife?

The clay trails which link St Austell town centre to Wheal Martyn, Bugle and the Eden Project, first opened in March 2005. The different terrains and distances take walkers, horse-riders, cyclists and wheelchair users on a variety of car-free routes throughout the area.

The accessibly designed tracks meander along the once white rivers of the area and take trekkers through wooded valleys, rhododendron-littered ex-clay tips, along the edge of disused pits and through the white-grey lunar landscape the area is so famous for.

The seven miles of car-free track, which make up the Pentewan Trail, begin in London Apprentice, just south of St Austell. The trail leads all the way to Pentewan Beach through Kings Wood (and is almost entirely flat).

The trail, which charts the old route of a narrow-gauge railway, which closed in 1916, runs along the St Austell river. Although not a major port, Pentewan operated as a small mineral export harbour but was mostly known as a fishing port.

Pentewan Quarry is most famous for its very fine Elvan stone, which was used to build a number of local churches including Lostwithiel, Fowey, Mevagissey and some parts of Antony House.

In 1985, blocks of the stone had to be reclaimed from the beach in order to restore the stonework on St Austell's Holy Trinity church.

Since the Second World War, Pentewan has become a popular caravan and camping site known as Pentewan Sands. Today, tents and caravans dominate the seafront during the summer where it's possible to pitch just metres from the sea (where the sound of the waves drowns out the snoring).

The seven-mile Goss Moor Trail takes walkers and riders through parts of the 480 acre National Nature Reserve – the largest surviving remnant of the mid-Cornwall Moors.

Goss Moor is believed to get its name from the Celtic word 'Cors' which means bog or marsh.

Today the area is home to a wealth of plant and animal species. Look out for bell heather, bristle bent, purple moor grass, the lesser butterfly orchid, hemlock water dropwort and the scarce yellow centaury Lucky twitchers might spy the nightjar, reed bunting, linnet, spotted flycatcher, bullfinch or song thrush. And... at nearby Screech Owl Sanctuary you'll find over 140 birds of prey and a flock of emus!

Long before the quiet car-free trails, Goss Moor was famous for its noisy traffic and long traffic jams.

As visitors heading to Newquay and the west hit the single carriageway and roundabout at Innis Downs, the tailbacks and bottlenecks on this stretch of the A30 were far from scenic. Adding insult to injury, the 14ft iron bridge carrying the Par to Newquay branch line, was a common crash site with lorries, unaware of their height, regularly attempting to drive under it, then blocking it.

In 2004, decisions were taken to widen the stretch of the A30 at Goss Moor, and the new Victoria Interchange opened at midnight on 9th May 2007. Lorries no longer have to negotiate the extremely low bridge and travel time to Newquay and the Eden Project has been reduced by well over 20 minutes.

Hundreds of thousands of visitors come to Cornwall to enjoy the Eden Project and many of its other, more traditional gardens. The St Austell area is not without a few of them.

The 30 acres of woodland and landscaping at Pinetum Park and Pine Lodge Gardens are a peaceful little gem, set back along the edge of the A390 at Holmbush.

Despite being relatively close to one of the area's main roads, the gardens are wonderfully quiet offering a lovely little idyll on the edge of St Austell.

In springtime the park is packed with snowdrops and in autumntime 80 different species of conifers, set in 4 acres, keep their colour as the wide collection of broadleaf trees shed their leaves. The gardens have over 6,000 species of plants (and a cracking little tea shop).

Head along the A390 from St Austell to St Blazey and on the left-hand side, just after the Britannia Inn, you'll see the entrance to Tregrehan Gardens.

Tregrehan has been home to the Carlyons since 1565. Records suggest that the family have been keen horticulturists since the beginning of the 17th century.

The estate's tree collection was planted during the 19th century by Jovey Carlyon, beneath which Gillian Carlyon's (1924-1987) most recent collection of camellias flourish.

Today Tom Hudson, Gillian's cousin, and his family live and work at the house and continue the horticultural traditions. At its floral peak during the spring, the 20-acre garden and 19th-century greenhouse offer a rich and exotic collection of plants, worthy of their links with Kew Gardens.

The 26 acres of woodland and walks at Wheal Martyn, Ruddlemoor, will take you on a journey through the history of china clay.

The heritage areas and interactive indoor exhibitions start at the very beginning of the clay industry and, as you step onto the viewing platform that looks out over a working china clay pit, they bring you right up to date.

The most recent visitor destination to be restored within the clay is built on the 13th-century settlement of Knightor. The name originally spelt 'Creyghter' means 'wrinkled land'.

After acquiring a small holding and some land from Imerys, just above the Eden Project, the owners of Knightor have renovated the buildings to make a winery, restaurant and shop.

Grapes from their 17,000 vines, which grow near Porthscatho, Looe and at Knightor itself, help to produce up to 8,000 bottles of award-winning wine every year (and we'll certainly raise a glass to that).

The most famous garden regeneration project to be created in Cornwall's clay country is undoubtedly the Eden Project.

At the time, the scaffolding used to build Eden's biomes held the Guinness World Record of being 'The World's Largest Free-Standing Scaffold Structure'. It needed 46,000 poles and would have stretched end-to-end for 230 miles (that's almost the distance between St Austell and London!).

When Eden opened on the 17th March 2000, the early morning Cornish mist blanketed the biomes, nobody could see a thing! Then as the sun rose over the horizon of the pit, it revealed what became known as the Eighth Wonder of the World (and there wasn't a dry eye in the house).

By June that year over 1 million people had visited.

Today, Eden continues to be one of the most inspiring post-mining regeneration projects on the planet. The Eden team is packed with the most passionate people you would ever wish to meet, without many of whom we could not have written and produced this book.

From the people I've met in the clay villages and at various events while researching this book, grandparents, parents and their children, I have always felt a strong sense that they all share an understanding of what really matters, of what is really important. A no-messing, no-wasting attitude that values family and friendship above all.

The clay villages are as handmade as the landscape that surrounds them. Numerous family homes in the clay were built by, and for, clay-working families. Community facilities were fund-raised for, then built and maintained in just the same way. Most proceeds from the clay carnivals, feast weeks and fund-raising events have paid for the church rooms, band clubs and recreation facilities. Yes, at times the architecture and landscape of this area is not always easy on the eye... but as Daphne du Maurier puts it, there is nothing ugly.

"Wild flowers straggle across the waste, seeds flourish into nameless plants, wandering birds from the moorland skim the lakes or dabble at the water's edge. Seagulls, flying inland, hover above the surface.

There is nothing ugly here... Cornishmen are wresting a living from the granite as they have done through countless generations, leaving nature to deal in her own fashion with forgotten ground, which, being prodigal of hand, she has done with a lavish and careless grace."

Image Credits: Clay Slip, James Ram. Sky tips – aerial view from Trenance Valley, China Clay History Society. Hensbarrow, Emma Mansfield. Clay Workers, China Clay History Society. Littlejohns, James Ram. Clay, James Ram. White Mountains, James Ram. Clay Strike, China Clay History Society. Hensbarrow, Emma Mansfield. Goss Moor, James Ram. Aerial of Pentewan in 1953, China Clay History Society. Clay Tips, China Clay History Society. Flatty and Pointy, John Sleeman. Carclaze Skytip, Emma Mansfield. Baal Clay lake, Emma Mansfield. View from Carloggas Downs, James Ram. St Austell Band, James Ram. Day break, James Ram. Tregonning Hill, Emma Mansfield. White Mountains, James Ram. Goss Moor Pylons, James Ram. Goonvean, Goonvean. Imerys, James Ram. Drinnick Pensioners event, China Clay History Society. Clay workers, China Clay History Society. Shift Captains, China Clay History Society. Clay worker, China Clay History Society. Monitor operator, James Ram. Tanks, James Ram. Balmaidens, China Clay History Society. Cornish unit, China Clay History Society. Trains at Rocks, James Ram. Charlestown, China Clay History Society. Charlestown Gig, Charlestown Rowing. Par Docks, China Clay History Society. Beach huts, Francis Frith Collection. Polkerris, Wiki Commons. Fowey, China Clay History Society. Red Arrows, Paul Colledge. St Dennis Clay Tips, China Clay History Society. Roche Carnival, James Ram. Summercourt Fair, St Enoder Parish Council. Bugle Band Festival, China Clay History Society. Bugle Band Festival, West of England Bandsmen's Festival. Bugle Band, James Ram. In the Square, Camborne Band. In the rain, James Ram. Treviscoe Male Voice Choir, China Clay History Society. Roche Carnival, James Ram. Carnival Float, Jennifer Pursall. Carnival Queens, Jennifer Pursall. Snail Creep, Clay Futures Project. Torchlight Carnival, James Ram. Pantomime, St Stephens Pantomime Group. China Café, Janet Shearer. Roche Football Pitch, James Ram. Chapel, China Clay History Society. Coombe Tea Treat, China Clay History Society. View from Carloggas Downs, James Ram. Building Bugle, China Clay History Society Carclaze Skytip, James Ram. Roche Rock, James Ram. Queens Head, China Clay History Society. Hell's Mouth, Steve Tanner. Longstone Speedway – Tempus Publications. Whitemoor Preaching Pit, Emma Mansfield. St Dennis, James Ram. Below Hensbarrow, James Ram. Retew, China Clay History Society. St Austell, China Clay History Society. St Austell viaduct, China Clay History Society. St Austell car train, David Tamblyn. Carlyon Hotel, China Clay History Society. Skytip, Emma Mansfield. Pentewan, Francis Frith Collection. Goss Moor, Cornwall Council.The Eden Project, The Eden Project.

Thank you to James Ram, John Sleeman, the China Clay History Society, the Francis Frith Collection, Steve Tanner, The Eden Project and all those who donated images from their personal and family photo albums. We could not have made this book look so great without them.

A personal thank you to Tom Barnecut, my partner in crime in creating this book project and the 50 Shades of Clay Exhibition. Michelle, Vicky and Jo who accompanied me on many a clay day out and clay trail. Paul, my designer, James for his company and photos, Martin Bates for his patient proof-reading and indexing. Rose, Charlotte and Oliver, thanks for your wise words and support. Thank you to Wheal Martyn. Thank you Clarice, Jennifer, Kathy and Thelma and all of you who contributed personal quotes and stories. Finally thanks, as always, to my family and friends for all their support and help as this family of little books gets bigger and bigger.

References and bibliography.

Catching Cornwall in Flight. **Ken Phillips, Cornish Hillside Publications, 1994.**
China Clay. **Charles Thurlow, Cornish Hillside Publications, 2007.**
China Clay, A Geologist's View. **Colin Bristow, 2006.**
China Clay from Devon and Cornwall. **Charles Thurlow, Cornish Hillside Publications, 2005.**
Clay Country Speedway. **Robert Bamford & Dave Stallworthy, Tempus, 2002.**
Cornish Place Names and Language. **Craig Weatherhill, Sigma, 2007.**
Cornwall, A Concise Encyclopaedia. **Mike Rule, Palores Publications, 2011.**
Cornwall Forever. **Cornwall Heritage Trust, 2000.**
Cornwall's China Clay Country. **Roger Fogg and Adrian Brown, Halsgrove, 2011.**
More Rhyme and Reason. **Clarice Westlake, Rhyme and Reason, 2010.**
St Austell Speedway, The Early Years 1949-1954. **Jeremy Jackson, Tempus, 2006.**
St Austell Through Time. **Valeria Jacob, Amberly, 2009.**
The Book of St Dennis and Goss Moor. **Kenneth Rickard, Halsgrove, 2004.**

The index refers to the text only - not photos.
Index entries refer to page numbers. Entries
are in letter-by-letter alphabetical order.